Isaiah Thomas

Vice in its proper Shape

Or, The wonderful and melancholy Transformation of several naughty Masters and Misses into those contemptible Animals which they most resemble in Disposition

Isaiah Thomas

Vice in its proper Shape

Or, The wonderful and melancholy Transformation of several naughty Masters and Misses into those contemptible Animals which they most resemble in Disposition

ISBN/EAN: 9783337192402

Printed in Europe, USA, Canada, Australia, Japan

Cover: Foto ©ninafisch / pixelio.de

More available books at **www.hansebooks.com**

FRONTISPIECE.

VICE

IN ITS

PROPER SHAPE;

OR, THE

Wonderful and Melancholy

TRANSFORMATION

OF SEVERAL

NAUGHTY MASTERS AND MISSES

INTO THOSE

Contemptible ANIMALS which they most resemble in Disposition.

Printed for the Benefit of all GOOD BOYS and GIRLS.

THE FIRST *WORCESTER* EDITION.

PRINTED at WORCESTER, *Massachusetts*,
BY ISAIAH THOMAS,
Sold at his BOOKSTORE, and by THOMAS
and ANDREWS in BOSTON.
MDCCLXXXIX.

INTRODUCTION.

IT was the opinion of the wife *Pythagoras*, and of some other philosophers, that the souls of men, women, and children, after their death, are sent into other human bodies, and sometimes into those of beasts and birds, or even insects; and that they hereby change their residence either to their advantage or disadvantage, according to their good or ill behaviour in their preceding state of existence. This singular opinion still prevails in some part of the Eastindies; and that to such a degree

degree that they make it criminal to put any animal to death: "For how do you know, say they, but in killing a sheep, a bird, or a fish, you murder your father, or your brother, or some other deceased friend or relation, whose soul may inhabit the body of the animal you so wantonly destroy?" An officer in the service of the Eastindia Company, and a particular friend of mine, had like to have lost his life by not paying a proper deference to this whimsical notion; for being some time in that part of the country, and happening to shoot a heron, he was immediately arrested and prosecuted for it by one or the natives. The man insisted

that

that the heron was inhabited by the soul of his father; and supported his point so much to the satisfaction of the court, that had it not been for the friendly assistance of a Jew, who appeared as the captain's advocate, he would certainly have been condemned. The Jew, allowed that what the plaintiff had asserted was strictly true, but pleaded in behalf of his client, that the soul of his, the said client's grandmother, resided in the body of a fish, which the said client had often seen and knew perfectly well; and that at the time when the heron was killed, the said heron was going to dart upon the said fish to devour it; so that

that the said client being strongly moved thereunto by his natural affection, instantly shot the said heron purely to save the life of his grandmother. This plea was admitted, and the captain was immediately discharged by order of the court. It is well for the reader that the captain escaped as he did: for if he had been hanged for murdering the heron, it is more than probable that it woud have been out of his power to have returned to England with that curious little treatise which I have now taken the pains to translate into English for the amusement of the little masters and misses of Great Britain.

It

INTRODUCTION.

It contains a diverting account of several naughty boys and girls, who, after their death (which was generally owing to their own folly) were degraded into such animals as they most resembled when alive. I cannot pretend to say who was the author; for his modesty was so great, that he has not inserted his name in the title page.

The captain tells me, it is the opinion of some of the Indian criticks, that he was an academy-keeper, who wrote for the instruction of his scholars; and of others, that he was a fond father who wrote for the entertainment of his children; but as it is very possible that both of them may be mistaken,

x INTRODUCTION.

I shall not presume to decide which of them have been so fortunate as to discover the truth in a matter of such evident importance.

I have only to observe, that as long proper names (such as those of the Indians) would have been too crabbed for most of my little readers, I have put myself to the amazing trouble of substituting English names in their room, which are expressive of the characters of the persons to whom they are applied. After humbly begging the author's pardon, for taking this liberty with his ingenious performance, I must desire all the masters and misses who read my translation of it, to be extremely careful to avoid all the crimes and follies which

which it was intended to correct; otherwife, if my friend the captain (who will probably hear of their ill behaviour) fhould happen to fpeak of it, when he makes another voyage to India, and it fhould by any means reach the ear of my author, we may perhaps have a fecond volume, containing a mortifying account of the furprifing and lamentable tranfmigrations of fome of the naughty boys and girls in England.

CHAP. I.

Of the wonderful Transmigration of Jack Idle *into the body of an ass.*

ONE morning after breakfast I took a walk into the fields with

with my seven dear children; which I did, not only for the benefit of their health, but as a reward for their good behaviour. They always obey me and their affectionate mother with the utmost cheerfulness; and I, in return, am always ready to indulge them as far as my duty and their interest will permit. When we had travelled about three miles from the city, where Divine Providence has fixed our abode, we came to a range of little tenements, or I should rather have called them sheds, over the midst of which (and it was likewise the largest) was fixed a board, on which was written in lofty capitals WAL*KINBE-HOL*D

HOL*DANDLE*ARN, which signifies, *Walk in, behold, and learn.* While I was musing upon this strange inscription, and wondering what curiosities there could be in such contemptible little huts, the door of the middlemost was suddenly opened by a Bramin, who with the greatest politeness and affability, desired us to walk in, assuring me, that notwithstanding the mean appearance of his little tenements, there were several things to be seen in them, which might contribute to the entertainment and instruction of my pretty fellow travellers. " I am, said he, " as you may perceive by my " habit,

---

* The captain informs that this inscription is in the language of the ancient *B—amins.*

"habit, a Bramin, and my name
"is *Wiseman*. All the time I can
"spare from the worship of my
"Maker, and the contemplation
"of that astonishing wisdom and
"beneficence which he has dis-
"played in his works of creation
"and providence, I cheerfully de-
"vote to the service of my fellow
"mortals, and particularly of the
"younger and unexperienced part
"of them. The most valuable
"service I can render them is to
"conduct them into the paths of
"virtue and discretion. For this
"purpose, having been gifted with
"the faculty of distinguishing
"those animals which are now
"animated by the souls of such
"human

"human beings as formerly de-
"graded themselves to a level with
"the unthinking brutes, I have
"taken the pains to provide a
"collection of beasts, birds, &c.
"most of which are inhabited by
"the souls of some naughty
"masters or misses, who died in
"the neighbourhood, and it is
"possible were not unknown to
"your little companions. It was
"a proverb among the ancient
"Bramins, that *Example is more
"powerful than precept,* and it is
"the common language of man-
"kind to this day, *I understand
"what I hear, but I believe what I
"see.* It would not be amiss
"therefore, if you were to ac-
"company

Vice in its proper Shape.

" company the young gentlemen
" and ladies into my little appart-
" ments, that they may be eye
" witnesses to the mortifying con-
" sequences of an ill spent and
" vicious life, even to those who
" have not arrived at the age of
" manhood."

We accepted the offer with the utmost gratitude, and eagerly inquired what we had to pay for admittance. But the good Bramin assured us, that he never made a traffick of the little wisdom he had to communicate, and that the most acceptable recompense we could make him, was, to bestow what we could prudently spare upon such real objects of charity as

B   might

might afterwards fall in our way:
—" For mercy and benevolence,
" said he, are the darling attri-
" butes of heaven, and those
" who are most distinguished for
" the practice of them, bear the
" nearest resemblance to their Mak-
" er, and will therefore receive
" the largest portion of his favour
" both in this world, and in that
" which is to come."

The first room we were conducted into was the habitation of a little
ass, who, as soon as we entered
the place, began to bray, and kick
up his heels, at a most violent
rate; but, upon the appearance
of Mr. Wiseman (which I have
before observed was the Bramin's
name,

name) he thought proper to compose himself, and stood as quiet as a lamb.——" This stubborn little
" beast said our kind conductor,
" is now animated by the soul of
" the late master *Idle*. In his life-
" time he possessed all the bad
" properties of the animal you see
" before you; so that, to speak
" the truth, he now appears in
" his proper shape. His rough
" coat of hair is a very suitable
" emblem of the ruggedness of his
" disposition; and his long and
" clumsy ears not only denotes his
" stupidity, but, as they afford a
" very secure and convenient hold
" to any one who has occasion to
" catch him when he runs loose in
" the

"the fields, they sufficiently inti-
"mate that he was always open
"to the ill advice of his play-
"fellows. If the meanest and
"most dirty boy in the neighbour-
"hood was in want of a compan-
"ion, or rather a tool, to assist
"him in his mischievous pranks,
"he had nothing to do but to
"make his application to *Jack
"Idle*; for foolish Jack (as they
"truly called him) was at the beck
"of every mischievous rogue; and
"when the mischief was done,
"he was always left, like a stupid
"ass as he was, to bear the burden
"of it. His father had money;
"and Jack's great pride was to
"be complimented by his raggamuffin

" muffin companions as the cook
" of the game. Once (I remem-
" ber it perfectly well) three
" bargemen's boys having a violent
" inclination to plunder a pippin
" tree, which was the property of
" farmer *Crusty*, they gave master
" Jacky such a tempting account
" of the wish'd for prize, and
" held forth so liberally in praise of
" his courage and ingenuity, that
" they prevailed upon him to be
" not only a party, but the com-
" mander in chief in this hopeful
" enterprize. But, as such ad-
" ventures generally terminate in
" the most mortifying disappoint-
" ment, the young plunderers
" were discovered by the farmer
" before

" before they had gathered half
" their booty. The three tar-
" paulins being at the bottom of
" the tree made their escape with-
" out much difficulty; but Jack,
" who, to support the dignity of

" his new command, had ascended
"almost

" almost to the top, was unfortu-
" nately taken prisoner. The
" consequence was, that his fa-
" ther (who had to deal with a
" wretch who was as crusty by
" nature as he was by name)
" after being obliged to pay ten
" times the value of the fruit,
" conducted his son to Mr. *Sharp*,
" the gentleman who had the trou-
" ble of his education, from whom
" he received a severe flogging in the
" presence of all his school fel-
" lows, as a very suitable reward
" of his stupid ambition. From
" this account of him you will
" naturally conclude that he was
" no great friend to learning;
" and, indeed, so remarkable was
" his

"his aversion to the useful arts of
"reading and writing, that his
"greatest improvement amounted
"only to an indifferent knowl-
"edge of the alphabet, and the
"poor accomplishment of being
"just able to scrawl his own
"name in characters which were
"scarcely legible. He was equally
"distinguished for his speed and
"fidelity when his parents sent
"him on an errand; for he could
"hardly make shift to saunter a
"mile in an hour, and when he
"arrived at the place of his desti-
"nation, he usually forgot three
"fourths of his message, and en-
"deavoured to supply the defect
"by some blundering tale of his
"own

"own invention. He was once
"dispatched by his father, in great
"haste, to a gentleman who lived
"not a quarter of a mile off, to
"request the favour of his com-
"pany, in half an hour's time, to
"settle matters with a grazier, of
"whom they had purchased several
"head of cattle; when Jack ar-
"rived at the gentleman's house,
"which he actually did in the
"short space of an hour and a
"half, he rubbed his eyes, and
"scratched his head, and inform-
"ed him that his father wanted
"him sadly, and that he must
"come directly to speak with the
"*brazier*, who, he said, had wait-
"ed for him above two hours. It
"was

"was very happy for his parents
"(whether they thought so or not)
"that Jack's sudden exit out of
"the world, in the thirteenth
"year of his age, effectually pre-
"vented him from bringing any
"material disgrace upon his fam-
"ily; which he certainly would
"have done, if he had lived to be
"his own master. The occasion
"of his death was as follows:——
"One morning, instead of making
"the best of his way to school,
"(which he was constantly or-
"dered to do) happening very
"luckily to be overtaken by *Tom
"Sharper*, and *Dick Lackwit*,
"they prudently agreed to avoid
"the intolerable drudgery of the
"hornbook,

"hornbook, by playing truant
"and indulging themselves in the
"profitable diversions of sitting all
"day on the bank of a lonesome
"brook to fish for minows; they
"had pretty good sport, as they
"called it, for the first hour; but
"then Mr. *Sharper's* line happening
"to be entangled among some
"large weeds, from which he could
"not disengage it as he stood
"upon the brink; and as he
"was naturally too great an adept
"in the science of self preserva-
"tion, to expose himself to dan-
"ger, when he could persuade an-
"other to supply his place; he
"requested the favour of master *Idle*
"to ascend a sloping tree which
"stood

"stood upon the bank, and from
"thence to descend gradually upon
"a hanging banch, the small end
"of which almost touched his
"line. Poor Jack was somewhat
"unwilling to venture upon the
"experiment; but a little more
"persuasion, which was supported
"by a few surly menaces, soon
"vanquished every objection. He
"accordingly ascended the tree;
"but when he attempted to seat
"himself upon the hanging branch
"the small twigs, upon which he
"stupidly fastened his hold for
"that purpose, suddenly gave way,
"and down he plunged into the
"middle of the brook, where, af-
"ter many eager and ineffectual
"struggles

Vice in its proper Shape. 29

" struggles to recover the bank,
" he sunk to the bottom, and rose
" no more. The last words he
" spoke were, *Oh! my dear father!*
" *my dear mother! I wish I had—*
" He meant I suppose, that he
" wished he had followed their
" good

"good advice; but the water,
"which ran very fast into his
"mouth, suddenly stopped his
"speech, and nothing more was
"heard but a faint bubbling in
"his throat, and two or three des-
"perate plunges at the bottom of
"the water, to preserve that life
"which fell a melancholy sacri-
"fice to his own folly and dis-
"obedience!—One would think
"that such a shocking catastrophe
"would be sufficient to subdue ten
"times the stubbornness and stu-
"pidity for which master *Idle* was
"so remarkable: But as we are
"too apt to forget the eager prom-
"ises, and laugh at the self con-
"demning reflections, which we
"have

"have made in the hour of diſtreſs,
"I need not mention it as a prod-
"igy, that the ſoul by which this
"little beaſt is animated, is ſtill
"infected with the ſame vicious
"diſpoſition, which diſgraced and
"puniſhed it, when it occupied
"the body of *Jack Idle*."

To convince us of the truth of what he ſaid, the good Bramin addreſſed himſelf to the aſs before us, and aſſured him that if he was ſincerely inclined to behave as he ought to do, and forſake the follies he had been guilty of in his former ſtate of exiſtence, he ſhould again have the honour to aſcend to the rank of human beings. But the ſtubborn little animal (who perfectly

fectly understood what he said) first leered at him with the most stupid resentment in the world, and then fell a braying and kicking with greater violence than when we first entered the room. "Soho! "said Mr. Wiseman, is that your "manners, my boy;"—and then giving him two or three hearty strokes, "well, well, said he, if "this is all the return I am to "have for my generous care of "you, I will certainly sell you "to the first sandman I see, who "will bestow upon you plenty of "drubbing, plenty of fasting, and "(what you will relish the worst "of all) a never failing plenty of "work."

CHAP. II.

An Account of the surprizing Transmigration of Master ANTHONY GREEDYGUTS, *into the Body of a Pig.*

THE next room into which we were conducted, contained a fat little pig, who, as soon as we had

had entered the door, began to cry *a week, a week, a week*, in such a squeaking tone as grated our ears in the most disagreeable manner: but as soon as Mr. *Wiseman* produced his wand, he lowered his pipes to a few sulky grunts, and then became as still as a mouse.—
" This young pig, said the venerable Bramin, is now animated by the soul of the late master *Greedyguts*, who died about two months ago, and has left a number of relations behind him in almost every town you can mention. Poor foolish youth, if he had been less fond of his belly, and more attentive to his book, and to the good advice of his parents, his soul would not have

been confined as it now is, in the body of that nasty, greedy, and noisy little animal which you see before you. But, to represent his character in its proper colours, he was always a hoggish little fellow, and disdained every other sort of labour but that of lifting his hand to his mouth. He loved eating much better than reading; and would prefer a tart, a custard, a plum-cake, or even a slice of gingerbread, or an apple, to the prettiest, and most useful little book you could present him with; so that if his parents had purchased a hundred books for him, one after the other, he would have readily parted with them to the first

first crafty boy he met with, who had any trash to spare by way of exchange. It cannot therefore be considered as a miracle, notwithstanding the extraordinary care and expense which his friends bestowed upon his education, that he always continued a blockhead, and was such a perfect dunce at eleven years of age, that instead of being able to read and write as a young gentleman ought to do, he could scarcely tell his letters. He was equally remarkable for his selfishness; for if he had twenty cheesecakes in his box, or his pockets full of oranges and apples, he would sooner have given a tooth out of his head than have parted

parted with one of them, even to his own brother or sister. The consequence was (and indeed what else could have been expected) that he was despised and hated by all his play fellows, and distinguished by the mortifying title of *Tony Pig* ; an animal which he perfectly resembled in his nastiness as well as greediness. For if he was dressed in the morning as clean as hands could make him, he would, by running into puddles and kennels, and rolling upon the ground, become as black as a chimney sweeper before noon ; and I sincerely believe that he thought it as great a punishment to have his hair combed, or to wash

wash his hands and face, as to be whipped; for he would cry and struggle as much to avoid the one as to escape the other. But, to ease his parents of their heavy apprehensions upon his account, and to rid the world of such a plague and disgrace, as he certainly would have been, if he

Vice in its proper Shape. 39

he had lived to years of maturity, kind death was pleased to dispatch him in the twelfth year of his age, by the help of a dozen penny custards, which he greedily conveyed down his throat at one meal, and thereby gorged his stomach, and threw himself into a mortal fever. After his exit

exit, his soul, as I have already informed you, was hurried into the body of this little pig; a station which perfectly corresponds with his disposition. Nay, so great is his stubbornness (which is another hateful quality in which he resembled the animal before you) that his punishment has not made the least alteration in his temper; for, if we were to get his soul replaced into a human body, upon his promise of immediate amendment, he will not submit even to make such a promise. To convince you that I have not misrepresented his character, I'll try the experiment immediately." Accordingly, the good Bramin asked him before us all,

all, if, upon the condition above-mentioned, he would leave off his greedy and selfish behaviour. To this he condescended, though with a visible reluctance, to grunt, *aye, aye.* " But how long will it be, said Mr. Wiseman, before you perform your promise?" *A week, a week, a week,* cried the pig. And how long will it be before you lay aside your nastiness, and maintain such a cleanly and decent appearance as becomes a gentleman?" *A week, a week,* said the dirty creature. " And how long will it be before you respect the good advice of your parents, and prefer the improvement of your understanding to the gratification of your appetite?"

tite?" *A week, a week, a week,* replied the stubborn little animal. "In short, said the worthy Bramin, if I were to repeat the same questions to him a month, or even a year hence, I should not prevail upon him to say *now*; but his constant answer would be, *a week, a week, a week.* I believe, therefore, that instead of reforming him (which is an event that would afford me the most sensible pleasure) we shall at last be forced to roast and eat him; for, as long as he continues in his present way of thinking, it is very certain that his existence can be of no service either to himself, or any one else." Thus, then, said he, I have

have troubled you with a particular account of this stupid little pig; and I sincerely hope that the story will prevail upon my young visitors to be cleanly in their appearance, temperate in their diet, and kind and obliging to every body; for whosoever pursues a contrary behaviour, is in reality a *hog*, though he bears the name of a gentleman.

CHAP. III.

The Transmigration of Miss Dorothy Chatterfast *into the Body of a Magpie.*

IN one corner of the room where poor *Tony Pig* was confined, hung a large cage, which was the prison of a pert young magpie. As soon as my son *Jacky*, who was the youngest of the company, and remarkably fond of birds, had saluted her by the well known appellation of *mag, poor mag*; she wagged her tail with surprising agility, and began to chatter in such an elevated tone, and with such a rapid pronunciation, that I was heartily glad when the kind Bramin commanded silence. "The body of this party coloured, loquacious bird, said he, is the involuntary residence of the late Miss Dorothy Chatterfast; who was a most notorious little gossip, and belonged to a family which is as numerous as that of the *Greedyguts*. To do her justice, she was a handsome little girl,

and

and as brisk and notable as any young miss in her neighbourhood. But to her own misfortune, and the unspeakable vexation of most persons who came within the sphere of her observation, her little tongue was as active as her hands. She learned to talk very early, and so speedy was her improvement in the art of prattling, that, before she was three years old, she could lisp out a tale in very intelligible language. Her parents were so unwise as to encourage her in this mischievous kind of ingenuity, not only from the pleasure they took in hearing how fast she learned to speak, but because they considered it as an infallible

fallible token that she would, in time, prove an excellent wit and a notable manager. It is not, therefore, to be wondered at, that she took a great deal of notice of every thing which passed in the family, and particularly in the kitchen. If any of the servants accidentally broke a teacup, or saucer, a glass, &c. or received an unexpected visit from some of their acquaintance, or relations, when her parents happened to be absent from home; she never failed to inform them of it, the first opportunity, with many aggravating circumstances of her own invention; for which they generally complimented her, by way of reward, with the flat-
tering

tering titles of *a good child, a sweet little dear,* and *a careful little girl.* By this officious impertinence she frequently got the servants reprimanded, and sometimes dismissed; so that by degrees they all began to fear and hate her. She was equally attentive to every trifle which happened at the school, where she was daily sent to learn the art of reading, and the use of her needle; for the moment she came home, and before she had well entered the parlour door, and made her courtesy, her little tongue began to rattle like a mill clack."——" Mamma, said she, Tommy Careless was flogged for tearing his book, Jackey Fidget

Vice in its proper Shape. 49

Fidget becaufe he was a naughty boy and would not fit ftill, Polly Giddybrains, for lofing her needle and thread paper, and, Lord blefs me! my ma'am was fo crofs, that fhe was going to put the nafty fool's cap on *my* head, only for mifcalling the firft first word in my lesson."—In short she was such a notorious telltale, that she was soon dignified by her school fellows with the honourable appellation of *Dolly Cagmag*. As she advanced in years, the habit grew upon her; and when she was old enough to be introduced into company, and go a visiting, she carried on the same mischievous and despicable trade abroad, in which she had met with such encouragement at home. Whatever she saw or heard in one place, she would be sure to report it in another; so that all the masters and misses who had the mortification to fall into her company, considered themselves

as

as under the malicious inspection of a meddlesome spy; which they had the more reason to do, because she seldom failed to embellish her informations with the recital of several unfavourable circumstances of her own invention." "Indeed, Mr. Wiseman, said Betsey, my youngest daughter, what you have told us is exactly true; for I have been in company with Miss Chatterfast several times, and I remember once in particular that when Master *Sprightly*, who was a merry young spark, had stolen a kiss from Miss *Patty Sweetlips*, though the poor young lady blushed as red as scarlet, and seemed to be greatly displeased at the freedom which

which had been taken with her, Miss Chatterfast was so mischievous as to represent her to all her acquaintance as a bold little hussey, who loved to be kissed by the young gentlemen. When poor innocent Patty was informed of the character which had been so unjustly fixed upon her, she was ashamed to stir out of doors, and laid it so much to heart I thought she would have cried her eyes out." "This was very unkind indeed, replied the good Bramin; and yet, I sincerely believe that all the mischief her tongue was guilty of, was more owing to her vanity and that talkative humour in which she had always been encouraged

couraged from her infancy, than to any real malice in her heart. She had been long accustomed to speak without thinking, and naturally imagined that her impertinent loquacity would be as much admired and applauded by other people as by her thoughtless parents. I have the satisfaction, however, to observe that you are perfectly sensible of her mistake, though she had not the good fortune to be so herself. If she had lived much longer, it is very probable that the many slights and affronts she must necessarily have met with, would have opened her eyes: For those who by their impertinent censures set the whole world at defiance,

fiance, may reasonably expect to find an enemy in every house they enter. But her meddlesome, inquisitive disposition proved to be the accidental means of shortening her days, before she had experience enough to correct it: for, one evening, Mr. *Kindly*, a wealthy merchant, indulged all the young masters and misses in the neighbourhood with a splendid ball at his own house: Miss *Chatterfast*, though she had at that time a severe cold upon her, was so desirous of embracing such a favourable opportunity of making her remarks upon the behaviour and different dresses of the company, and thereby furnishing herself with an ample
stock

stock for conversation, that she could not be prevailed upon by her too indulgent parents to spend the evening at home. The consequence was such as might naturally have been expected. By first over heating herself at the ball, and afterwards exposing herself to the night air in her return home, her cold, (which was bad enough before) suddenly increased into a violent fever which hurried her to the grave in the short space of five or six days. Though her untimely death excited the transient pity of most of her acquaintance, very few of them, I believe, were really sorry to part with her. But notwithstanding that violent
propensity

propensity to exercise her tongue, which she too frequently indulged to the vexation of her neighbours, she had a large fund of good nature at the bottom; so that I am in hopes that she will soon be restored to the rank of human beings, and have an opportunity of employing her speaking faculties with greater discretion, and in a more agreeable manner than she did before. Her former loquacity (as I have already observed) was almost entirely owing to that vanity and want of thought, in which she had been too much encouraged by the simple fondness of her parents; but the low station in which she now appears, will probably

probably teach her to be more humble and considerate, and of consequence to check that talkative humour which in her past lifetime formed the most remarkable part of her character." Poor mag (who, I suppose, understood every word the Bramin said) wagged her tail a little, as we left the room, but did not think proper to utter a single chatter.

CHAP.

58 *Vice in its proper Shape.*

CHAP. IV.

The Transmigration of Master Stephen Churl, *into the Body of a little Cur.*

IN the next apartment we entered, we saw a little snarling cur, who

Vice in its proper Shape. 59

who immediately saluted us with a surly grin, and barked and yelped as if he would have torn the house down. He was indeed very securely chained to a small kennel; but my daughter Betsey happening to venture too near him, he snapped at her and tore her apron. " Take care, miss, said Mr. Wiseman, and keep out of his reach; for though he is but a cur, he is very mischievous. His body is the contemptible residence of the soul of the late Master *Churl*. Poor miserable youth! he was a wrangler from his infancy; and his litigious temper gave him as just a title to the name of *Churl* as his birth. Even when

when he was a child in arms, he was such a peevish and noisy little brat, that his mamma could not find a woman who would undertake the trouble of nursing him; and as soon as he was able to speak and run alone, he began to wrangle with his brothers and sisters, upon the most trifling occasions, and seldom forgot to support his argument by exerting his little hands and heels with the most malicious activity; so that to mortify his pride, and give a check to his illnature, they bestowed upon him the disgraceful title of young *Kick and Cuff*. Poor Stephen, however bid defiance to all their ridicule,

ridicule, and was so far from being reclaimed by it, that his turbulence increased in proportion to his strength and stature. He was afterwards as quarrelsome at school as he had been at home; and in every party at taw, or trap ball, or any other innocent diversion in which he happened to be engaged, he was always remarkable for disturbing the game by his frivolous disputes: Nay, when he was only a looker on, he would betray his wrangling impertinent temper, by calling out, "such a one does not play fairly; such a one counts too many; and such a one goes in before his turn."

turn." The usual reward he received for his trouble was, a handsome drubbing, sometimes from his master, but more frequently from his school fellows. He was equally notorious for his great forwardness to give a challenge, upon the slightest provocation, and very often from mere wantonness; and sometimes he would very unfairly begin an engagement without giving any previous notice, that he might make sure of the first blow. But his strength and skill being unequal to his pretensions, the many mortifying defeats he received, soon taught him the despicable cunning of
assaulting

assaulting none but those, who, he believed, were either too weak to contend with him, or too cowardly to stand in their own defence. The speedy consequence of such a dirty conduct was, that the bigger boys despised and laughed at him, and those who were less than himself, carefully shunned his company; so that at last poor wrangling Stephen, for want of playfellows, had no other diversion left for him, but to take a solitary ramble through the fields. His parents being informed of the disagreeable situation into which he had brought himself, and what a shy reception he met with

with from all the boys in the neighbourhood, thought it adviseable, after giving him a strict caution to behave in a more peaceable manner for the future, to remove him to a genteel boarding school, at a distance from home. If he had thought proper to follow their advice, and make a diligent use of the excellent instructions he received from his new teachers, he might afterwards have cut a shining figure in the world; but, as what is bred in the bone, seldom gets out of the flesh, so it fared with *Stephen Churl.* Though he was a little reserved at first, as being entirely among strangers,

a

a short acquaintance with them made him very familiar—the affability and good nature with which they listened to every thing he said, soon encouraged him to be pert; and from pertness he proceeded to open rudeness and ill manners—until at last happening to be very mildly reprimanded by one of the young gentlemen, whose tenderness he misconstrued into cowardice, he commenced hostilities, as usual, by giving him an unexpected blow on the face. But his antagonist being possessed of as much spirit as politeness, returned the compliment in an instant; and conducted the engagement

66 *Vice in its proper Shape.*

gagement on his side with such vigour and activity, that our hero soon retired from the field of battle heartily drubbed, to make his complaint to the master, who, after a minute inquiry into all the circumstances

cumstances of the fray, thought proper to reward him for the unnecessary trouble he had given himself, with the severest flogging he had ever received in his life time. Thus mortified and disgraced, the unfortunate *Stephen* resolved upon an elopement; but, being ashamed to return to his parents, he rambled through the fields and woods, and scrambled over hedges and ditches, until at length having torn his clothes to rags, and being almost ready to perish with hunger, he eagerly lifted himself into a gang of gypsies, and supped very heartily upon the remains of a roasted cat.

The

The intolerable hardships he suffered, and the coarse fare he was obliged to put up with in this new situation, together with the frequent bangs and thumps which he received from the

younger part of his strolling comrades,

comrades who were as quarrelsome and mischievous as himself, but abundantly more robust, soon broke his heart; so that he died in a barn, and was buried, like a beggar, at the expense of a little country parish." While the Bramin was concluding the history of Master *Churl*, my son *Jackey*, whose temper was rather too fiery, looked very sheepish; which his sister *Betsey* observing, and easily guessing the cause of it, she desired him with a good natured smile, when we were leaving the room, to think on poor *Stephen*, and be sure to take warning.

CHAP.

CHAP. V.

The comical and mortifying Transmigration of little Monsieur Fribble *into the Body of a Monkey.*

AFTER we had taken our leave of Master *Churl,* we were conducted

conducted into the apartment of Mr. *Pug*, a chattering young monkey, who, as soon as he saw us whipt his little hat under his arm in a crack, and seating himself upon his backside, welcomed each of us into the room by several ceremonious nods, which were intended to supply the place of a bow, and were accompanied by such a noisy affected grin, that it was impossible for us to forbear laughing—" This comtemptible animal, said Mr. *Wiseman*, is inhabited by the little soul of the late Master *Billy Fribble*, a young gentleman of French extraction, whose friends came and settled in the country about fifty

fifty years ago. His play fellows dignified him with the humorous title of *the little Monsieur*, not so much on account of his diminutive stature, as for that trifling and finical behaviour which distinguishes the least respectable, though, by many thoughtless persons, the most admired part of the French nation. As neither his bodily nor mental faculties were very vigorous, his childhood was remarkable only for a certain effeminate vivacity, which continually displayed itself in such a noisy and insignificant prattling, as was very tiresome and disagreeable to every body in the house.

house. When he grew older, he added to his former loquacity the most passionate fondness for fine clothes; so that in the twelfth year of his age, he became as complete a top as ever eyes beheld. He wore upon his head a macaroni hat about the size of a small tea saucer; his coat, which scarcely had any skirts to it, was of the most glaring colour he could fix upon; and his hair, which was plaistered over with powder and pomatum, was tied behind in a large club, which hung swagging upon his shoulders like a soldier's knapsack. Thus elegantly dressed, he strutted along the

the streets with a large stick in his hand about a foot taller than himself, and a small cutteau de-chasse by his side, which he could handle with as much dexterity as his pen; an instrument in the use of which he had made such a contemptible proficiency, that it required as much acuteness to discover the meaning of his aukward scrawl, as to explain the hieroglyphick characters of the ancient Egyptians. What still increased the obscurity of every thing which Monsieur *Fribble* undertook the trouble of penning, was that, excepting when he wrote his own name, he had a method of spelling

ing which was peculiar to himself. He was equally famous for his skill in the useful science of numbers; for though, during the space of seven or eight years, he devoted to it a considerable part of that lingering time which he was forced to spare from his private diversions in school hours, the sum total of his improvement was, that he was scarcely capable of casting up the contents of a shoemaker's little bill. His highest ambition was, in the first place, to furnish himself with a large collection of complimentary phrases, which he had seldom discretion enough to apply with any tolerable

ble propriety; and, in the next, to complete himself in the polite art of dancing, in which he so far succeeded as to be able to skip about with the most regular agility, though he never had a sufficient share of good sense to be able to dance with gracefulness. Thus accomplished, he excited the admiration of every silly coquette, and the envy of every fluttering coxcomb; but by all young gentlemen and ladies of understanding he was heartily despised as a mere civilized monkey. He performed every thing by imitation; and he imitated nothing (unless he was forcibly compelled to it)

by

by which a rational being may be diftinguifhed from a brute animal. But the fpecies of imitation in which he moft delighted, was that which, in the vulgar ftyle, is called *mocking*; for he was not poffeffed of a fufficient ftock of ingenuity to be (what he very frequently attempted to be) a clever mimick. If any of his fchoolmates happened to be afflicted with an impediment in their fpeech, an accidental lamenefs, or the like; he had the mean barbarity to endeavour to aggravate the misfortune by a coarfe imitation, which generally turned the whole ridicule upon himfelf. He once had

78 *Vice in its proper Shape.*

had the impudence to practise his mockery upon a worthy gentlemen in the neighbourhood, who was so unfortunate as to be unable to speak without stuttering. The gentleman happening to pass by Mr. *Fribble's* door, at which our little mon-

sieur

fieur was then standing with a magpie in his hand." "*Bi-bi-bill*, said the good man (after inquiring very civilly how he did) has that pretty ma-ma-mag learned to ta-ta-talk?" "Ye-ye-yes, replied the saucy fop, be-be-better than you do, or else I would wring his head off." "This rude and impertinent answer, which at first excited the laughter of some of the by-standers, soon gave them a very mean opinion of him, and he was afterwards despised by every sensible person, as a mischievous, unthinking coxcomb. What aggravated his punishment was, that he had so frequently indulged

dulged himself in the ungenerous and silly practice of mocking the imperfect pronunciation of others, that at last he himself contracted such a habit of stuttering as he could never leave off. This gave such a poor recommendation to the nonsensical things he was continually saying, that he became the object of ten times the ridicule which he had endeavoured to inflict upon those who had a *natural* impediment. What was pitied in them as a misfortune, was despised in him as an ill-acquired and consequently a vicious imperfection; and therefore every one was willing to
increase

Vice in its proper Shape. 81

increase the mortifying smart of it, and keep alive the conscious shame he felt of wearing a fool's cap which was entirely of his own making. This vexatious, and in some degree, vindictive ridicule to which he was daily exposed, and which, in time, he might have softened and disarmed by an humble and penitent deportment, gave such an insupportable wound to his foolish pride, that he soon absconded from company, and died of a broken heart. That his soul might afterwards occupy such a station as would be most suitable to his character, it was sentenced to inhabit the body of

F that

that finical, grinning, and mischievous little mimick with four legs, which you now behold before you." As soon as the Bramin had finished his story, poor *pug* (who seemed to retain all the little pride of Monsieur *Fribble*) grinned, chattered, and skipped about with a ridiculous resentment which was mingled with evident marks of fear; until at last, having agitated himself into a perfect passion, he made a hasty spring at his keeper, which, to his own abashment, and the laughter of my young companions, was as suddenly checked by a small chain that secured him to the floor.

CHAP.

Vice in its proper Shape. 83

CHAP. VI.

The dismal Transmigration of Master Tommy Filch, into the Body of a Wolf.

AS soon as we had lifted up the latch to enter into the
next

next apartment, we were immediately alarmed by a horrid howling; which upon opening the door we discovered to be the savage musick of a lusty young wolf, who looked as fierce as if he would have torn every one of us to pieces. But a strong chain confined his fury to one corner of the room; so that we could venture pretty near him without any danger of feeling the strength of his jaws. "This plundering and voracious animal, said the Bramin, who has been accustomed to gratify his appetite at the expense of all the farmers in the neighbourhood, is inhabited by the soul of the late Master *Filch*, who, as you will find by the sequel of the

the story, is now placed in a station which is perfectly suitable to his character. His very infancy was disgraced by a natural propensity to fraud and rapine; for as soon as he could talk plain enough to be understood, the chief employment of his tongue was to tell as many stories as his little head was capable of inventing; and that his hands might come in for their share of mischief, he never failed to make a property of all the sugar, fruit, tarts, &c. which the carelessness of the servants had left within his reach. If his parents had been wise enough to chastise him for his little roguery, they might have nipped it

it in the bud; but they were so
imprudently fond, that they not
only neglected to administer the
discipline of the rod, but made
his falsehood and pilferings the
constant subject of their merri-
ment. They considered his
faults as trivial, because they
were the faults of a child; not
reflecting that if the seeds of
vice are suffered to grow, they
will in a shorter time than is
commonly imagined, take such
deep root in the heart, that it
will be scarcely possible to erad-
icate them. Experience, however, soon undeceived them; for
when little *Filch* was eight or
nine years old, though he had
plenty of fruit at home, they
had

had the mortification to be informed that he was making daily incurfions into every poor man's garden in the neghbourhood. The confequence of thefe repeated complaints was fometimes a fevere reprimand, and fometimes as fevere a flogging; but neither the one nor the other were able to produce a reformation, though it is very probable, that if they had been applied in time, they might have been applied to better purpofe. From robbing orchards he foon proceeded to the raifing private contributions on his fchool fellows. Sometimes he defrauded them at play: fometimes he picked their pockets; and very frequently

frequently he stole their books, or money, out of their desks and boxes: and, as it is the study of every wicked boy to maintain the appearance of honesty as long as he is able, as soon as the robbery was discovered he was the first person to exclaim against it, which he did in the bitterest terms, and to prevent a long and circumstantial inquiry after the author of it (which he suspected would not terminate in his favour) he impudently pretended to have been an eye witness of the fact, and then boldly charged it upon one or another of his school mates, who he knew had neither skill nor spirit enough to contradict his evidence in a satisfactory

satisfactory manner. By this means the bashful innocent was frequently punished instead of the guilty. But as bad boys are seldom able to conceal their faults long from the eye of justice, young *Filch* was soon detected in his wickedness, and being considered as a dangerous person, whose bad example might have a pernicious effect upon his play fellows, he was first corrected with all the severity he deserved, and then sent home to his parents. In this disgraceful manner he was dismissed from every school in the country, 'till at last, though he was only thirteen years old, there was not a single academy into which he could be admitted

admitted upon any terms whatever. But this was not the worst effect of the ill character he had acquired: for as no one is willing to introduce a lad of bad reputation into his house, there was not a tradesman of any credit to be found who would venture to take him as an apprentice, though a large premium was offered for that purpose. His parents, therefore, were under the disagreeable necessity of keeping him at home; but having little or nothing for him to do, he soon fell into bad company, who in as short a time gave him a perfect relish for the scandalous and expensive amusement of gaming and tippling. His finances, though sufficiently plentiful for a youth of his age, were by these destructive means so much encumbered with little debts, that to maintain a worthless credit among his worthless companions, he formed the wicked resolution of taking money from his father and mother without their knowledge. The success of his first attempt (in which he was not discovered, because he was not suspected to be capable of so much baseness) encouraged him to a second; and the success of his second attempt encouraged him to greater extravagances and more expensive risk than he had ventured upon before. But his wickedness, which in the former instances had been wrong-

wrongfully charged upon the servants of the family, being at last detected, and his parents taking him very severely to task on account of such an abandoned and depraved conduct, he left them in a fit of anger and remorse, and became a thoughtless and unhappy wanderer; in this situation, falling one evening into a company whose mirth and gaiety greatly delighted him, and whose genteel appearance led him to suppose they were gentlemen, though in reality they were no other than highwaymen, he was prevailed on in an unguarded moment, when heated with liquor, to make an incursion with this infamous

Vice in its proper Shape. 93

mous banditti, and actually stopped a gentleman and demanded his money; fortunately, how-

ever for this unhappy youth, the gentleman was an old school fellow, and making himself known to him, with much intreaty prevailed on him immediately to leave

leave the company of those desperate adventurers, and totally to abandon a mode of life so shockingly wicked in itself, and so dreadfully fatal in its consequences.

"But from the idle and dissipated manner in which he had spent his time, he had contracted an unconquerable habit of indolence, and a rooted aversion to business; in this frame of mind, the army became his last resource, into which he entered as a common soldier, but after a short time his itch for pilfering returning, he could not refrain from making free with some money with which he was intrusted by his officer; being

Vice in its proper Shape. 95

ing detected, he was punished with that rigorous severity with which thefts in the army usually are, and being afterwards thrown into the Savoy prison, to prevent a repetition of his crime, he died there in a few days of his wounds in the utmost misery." When

the

the Bramin had finished this melancholy tale, the poor wolf, as if he was conscious how nearly it concerned him, heightened the horrour with which it had filled us by such a mournful and terrifying howl, as made us heartily glad to quit the room."

CHAP.

Vice in its proper Shape. 97

CHAP. VII.

Of the wonderful Transmigration of Master Richard Rustick, *into the Body of a Bear.*

IN the next apartment into which Mr. *Wiseman* conducted us, we saw the cub of a bear, who lay

upon the floor to which he was
chained, without having the good
manners to rife when we entered;
but when the Bramin applied his
wand to young Bruin's buttocks,
he heaved up his fhaggy hide with
a kind of lazy refentment, and
faluted us with a reluctant grin
and a favage growl, which plainly
intimated that he did not think
himfelf much beholden to us for
our company. " This young
brute, faid our conductor, is
animated by the foul of the late
mafter *Ruftick*, of clownifh memory. His father was a gentleman of rank and fortune, and
greatly beloved and refpected by
all his acquaintance; and if his
fon Richard had poffeffed the
fame

same virtues and accomplishments, he might afterwards have enjoyed his title and estate with equal comfort and reputation. But as merit does not go by inheritance, like house and land, young *Rustick*'s character was entirely the reverse of his father's. He was of an awkward clumsy make; and the heaviness of his disposition, and the coarseness of his manners perfectly corresponded with the shape of his body. Though he was sent to school very early, and put under the care of the best instructors which the country afforded, he was a considerable time before he could tell his letters, and much longer before he could
read

read with tolerable accuracy: and even then he pronounced every thing with such a clownish accent and such a drawling tone, that any stranger would have taken him for a young country bumkin, who had been used to follow the plow tail, and not for the son and heir of a wealthy gentleman. He was equally eminent for his neatness and dexterity in the art of penmanship; for, even when he was twelve years old, if you had seen the letter which he then sent to his mamma without the knowledge of his master, it was wrote so crooked (i. e. not from side to side as it ought to have been, but from corner to corner)

corner) and the strokes were all so coarse and uneven, and the whole of the letter so awkwardly spelt, and so unmercifully blotted and bedawbed, that you would have thought it had been the elegant epistle of *Tony Clodhopper* to his grandmother *Goody Linsey Woolsey*. As for his mamma, poor gentlewoman! when she first opened it, she thought it had been sent to her by some impudent shoe black or chimney sweeper; but when she had directed her eyes to the bottom and read (though not, I assure you, without the greatest difficulty)—" *from yr, loven ind respactfle sun, Rickard Rostick*," she was so much oppressed with shame

shame and vexation, that she tore the letter into a thousand pieces, and was ready to burst into tears. He was alike remarkable for the politeness of his manners, and his agreeable address; for he had such a treacherous memory, though he had been frequently reminded of the propriety and indeed the necessity of observing those little punctilios of good behaviour, that he seldom remembered when any company entered the room in which he happened to be sitting, either to rise from his chair or take off his hat; and when he was told of it either by his parents or his master, he would bounce up, and snatch of his hat in such an awkward

awkward hurry, grinning and leering the whole time, that you would have thought he had just started from a dream; and even then he would generally forget to finish the rude ceremony by making one of his ducking bows. It is true, indeed, he had been under the hands of a dancing master; but notwithstanding the utmost care and assiduity of his teacher, who was esteemed a very excellent one; he was never able to perform a whit better than he does in his present shape. In short, you might as well have kept a hog in training for Newmarket races, or an ox for his majesty to ride upon at a grand review, as have attempted to
initiate

104 *Vice in its proper Shape.*

initiate master *Dicky Rustick* in the elements of politeness and good breeding. With such a delicate disposition, and such amiable talents, you will readily perceive that he must have been a most agreeable play fellow. His favorite diversion was that which has been distinguished by

the

the vulgar, by the well known name of *Pully Hawly*, in which he so much excelled that whenever he was invited by the young gentlemen and ladies in the neighbourhood to play with them, he generally rewarded their civility by tearing their coats or pulling their clothes off their backs before he returned home; so that at last they bestowed upon him, by general consent, the honourable title of *'Squire Bruin*. It must, however, be acknowledged that he was a youth of such impartial justice, that he shewed as little favour to his own clothes as to those of *other* people; for what with climbing up old trees, and ram-

rambling over hedges and ditches, to seek for birds nests, he commonly appeared by dinner time, how well soever he had been dressed in the morning, in as ragged a coat as he wears at present. It must also be remarked, that if the young gentlemen and ladies soon grew weary, as indeed they did, of such a rough play fellow, he, in *his* turn, was as willing to leave *their* company, as they were to be rid of *his*; for his chief delight was to associate with such vulgar boys and girls as were of the same rugged disposition as himself. With these he could pull and hawl and romp and tear as long as he pleased; and the more active

active he became in this raggamuffin species of diversion, the more they relished his company. But, upon occasion, he could fight as well as play: I mean when he either was provoked to it by his equals, or tempted to it by the hopes of defrauding of their little property those who he knew had neither strength enough nor courage to resist him. But whatever was his motive either for *beginning* or suffering himself to be *drawn* into an engagement, he was very far from confining himself to any rules of honour, or to the established laws of war; for instead of boxing fairly, he would kick, pull hair, bite, and scratch most unmercifully, and

never

108 *Vice in its proper Shape.*

never fail to take every advantage of his antagonist after he had brought him to the ground. For these reasons he was soon dignified with the nick name of *Dick Bear*, even by the vulgar

boys in the streets; and most of them afterwards took care never to engage with him unless when
there

there were several other boys present to see fair play. One would think that such a rough hewn and slovenly mortal as we have been describing would have had little regard for any delicacies in the eating way. But whoever draws such a conclusion in favour of our hero, *Dicky Rustick*, is greatly mistaken; for I can assure you that he had as nice and dainty a tooth as any lady in the land. Though his father always kept a handsome table, it afforded scarcely any thing which was good enough for the palate of Master *Richard*. Nothing would go down with him but tarts, custards, and the most costly cakes and puddings;

for

110 *Vice in its proper Shape.*

for as to good roast and boiled meat and plain and wholesome pies or dumplings, he would turn up his nose at them as if they were fit only for vagabonds and beggars. Nay, even to this very hour, and in his present clumsy shape, he is almost as dainty as ever; for he is re-

markbly

markably fond of honey, and if permitted would often expose his shaggy head and his eyes to the resentment of the bees, by disturbing their hives to rob them of their delicious store. It was his fondness for niceties of every kind which shortened his days, and eased his parents of their apprehensions for a son who, if he had lived, would have been a continual plague and disgrace to them; for on the day when he entered into the fourteenth year of his age, being indulged rather more than common, he devoured such a quantity of the richest tarts, that his stomach could not digest them; so that he soon fell into a violent fever, which

which in a few days hurried his unworthy foul out of the body of a young country 'fquire (for fuch he would have been) into the carcafs of this hairy and awkward young monfter which now ftands before you. He fo well underftands what I have been faying, and is fo much vexed at the character I have given of him, which he knows to be a very juft one, that if you will promife to quit the room and leave him to himfelf he will pleafure you with one of his beft dances before you go."—Accordingly after thanking the Bramin for the account he had given us, we all promifed to leave Mr. *Bruin* to his own

own meditation; upon which, after taking two or three sulkey rounds, the young savage reared himself upon his buttocks, and shuffled a saraband which lasted a few minutes. When he had finished his dance he swaggered down again upon his fore paws, and by a sullen growl seemed to claim the performance of our promise, an indulgence which we very readily granted him.

CHAP. VIII.

Of the astonishing Transmigration of Miss Abigail Eviltongue *into the Body of a Serpent.*

IN the next apartment we saw a large wire cage, in which the Bramin told us he had a bird which was something different from the common

common ones; and so indeed it was, for upon my eldest daughter's going near to see it, she was startled by a large serpent which darted itself against the wires, and hissed and sissed as if it would have stung us all to death in an instant. It was however, a very beautiful creature of the kind, and as the sun then shone very bright, the golden and silver streaks upon its azure skin made a very splendid appearance. My youngest son wanting to go and stroke it;—" No, my pretty boy, said the good Bramin; if you have any value for yourself, you will always keep out of the reach of such creatures as these, and of all such who resemble the young lady
by

by whose soul this serpent is animated. I say *young lady*, because the serpent before you is indeed animated by the soul of the late Miss *Abigail Eviltongue*. The family of the *Eviltongue*, (I dare say you have heard of them) is extremely numerous; for there are some, and indeed too many of them, in every town, and, I believe in every village in the country. Miss *Abigail*, the young lady I am speaking of, had as just a title to the name, and supported the character of her family with as much exactness as any one amongst them; for her tongue was remarkably active, and spared the reputation neither of friend

friend nor foe. She was, it is true, a very handsome girl, and the charms of her person would have procured her many admirers if they had not been disgraced by her natural propensity to slander and defamation. In her very infancy, as soon as she could speak to be understood, she began with telling fibs of the servants, and very frequently of her brothers and sisters; for which, you may be certain, they all despised her very heartily. But as she was too much encouraged in this hateful practice by her parents, instead of being severely flogged for it, as she ought to have been, she set the frowns and sneers of the others

others at open defiance; and the more they resented her little malice the more eager she was to gratify it by loading them with all the falsehoods she was capable of inventing. In proportion as she grew older, this mischievous habit increased upon her; and when she was big enough to go a visiting, she indulged it abroad with as much freedom as she had been used to do at home; so that, in a short time, there was scarcely a young miss or master in the neighbourhood whose character she had not attempted to injure. What made her slanders the more odious was, that she generally vented them under a pretence of

the

the greatest friendship and respect for the persons to whom she related them, and with great seeming pity for those whose reputation they were intended to destroy. She had likewise the malicious cunning to say many trifling things in praise of the objects of her censure; that by thus assuming an appearance of the strictest impartiality, and of the sincerest good nature, she might more easily gain credit to the bad things she said afterwards. By such artifices as these she frequently succeeded with the innocent and the unwary, and set one acquaintance and even one friend against another, without any sort of advantage

to

to herself but the mere pleasure of making mischief. Another trick which she often employed for that purpose, was to examine into a young gentleman or lady's constitutional foibles (for we all have some) and when she had discovered these, to go immediately to the person and tell him or her, that master or miss *such a one* had publickly ridiculed him for those very failings; by these means she was almost certain to be believed without any farther inquiry; for every one, even upon the slightest hint, will readily suspect that those things have been said of him, which he most wishes to be concealed, because he is conscious they are

really

really true; he will seldom trouble himself to inquire into the veracity of the tale bearer, lest he should be reduced to the necessity of defending himself on his weakest side. For a similar reason, when Miss *Abigail* had a mind to flatter any person (which she frequently would, to answer the purposes of her malice) she always commended him for those particular good qualities, or accomplishments which she knew he most valued himself for, or chiefly wished to have the credit of; because she was sensible that by this method she effectually retained his own vanity as her advocate for whatever she said afterwards. Nay, I have been informed by
one

one who knew her perfectly well, that, young as she was, she sometimes carried her artifice so far as to begin a dispute with the person she intended to deceive, and after a little sharp altercation *pro and con* to flatter his vanity by gradually giving up the argument, and at last yielding him a

victory,

victory, which gave him the more pleasure, because he thought it to be entirely owing to the invincible strength of his judgment. But she had another fault, which, if possible, was still more odious, than any of those already mentioned—viz. to revile and backbite those from whom she had received the greatest favours; for as she was too proud to own herself to be under obligations to any person, so to prevent others from taking notice of them, as she imagined to her disadvantage, she would represent every obligation she had received from her friends to be either of the most trifling consequence, or to have been bestowed from selfish and

def-

124   *Vice in its proper Shape.*

despicable motives. Such was
the temper and behaviour of Miss
Abigail, who was a wretched
complication of malice, low

cunning and ingratitude : It is
therefore no wonder that every
person of sense and character was
careful to avoid her company,
and

and that she was detested by
many, and despised even by those
who wished her well. In short,
the general contempt to which
she had exposed herself, and the
severe mortifications she met
with from time to time, gave
such killing wounds to her pride,
that after pining and wasting

away

away with shame and vexation for the space of several months, she at last broke her heart and gave up the ghost, in the seventeenth year of her age. After her death her contemptible soul was immediately hurried into the body of this venomous serpent, where it still retains its former malice and cunning."—When the Bramin had finished his story, the serpent, as if she understood and resented what had been said, writhed about and hissed at him as if she could have stung his eyes out.

We afterwards visited several other apartments, and saw a young tyger, a fox, a badger, &c. each of which was animated by the soul of some naughty child, who very nearly

nearly resembled him in temper. But as I have perhaps, already carried my treatise to such a length as will tire the eyes and the patience of my little readers, it is proper to bring it to a conclusion. I will, therefore, take my leave of them for the present, with observing that in one of the rooms we visited, we saw a pretty little parrot, in a gilt cage, who was perpetually talking, but did not understand the meaning of one single word he said. " This noisy bird, said the good Bramin, is inhabited by the soul of the late master *Gabble*, who was remarkable for two faults. He always spoke without thinking, and read a great deal with so little attention, that he made

no

no farther improvement in knowledge than if he had never read at all. He devoured every thing, but digested nothing." If any of my readers happen to be of the same disposition, they may survey the gilt covers of this little treatise with as much advantage as they will peruse the contents of it.

FINIS.

www.ingramcontent.com/pod-product-compliance
Lightning Source LLC
Chambersburg PA
CBHW030902170426
43193CB00009BA/715